Badgers

Julie Murray

Abdo
NOCTURNAL ANIMALS
Kids

abdopublishing.com

Published by Abdo Kids, a division of ABDO, PO Box 398166, Minneapolis, Minnesota 55439.
Copyright © 2018 by Abdo Consulting Group, Inc. International copyrights reserved in all countries.
No part of this book may be reproduced in any form without written permission from the publisher.

Printed in the United States of America, North Mankato, Minnesota.

102017

012018

 THIS BOOK CONTAINS
RECYCLED MATERIALS

Photo Credits: iStock, Minden Pictures, Shutterstock, ©User:Quintucket p.7 / CC-BY-SA 3.0

Production Contributors: Teddy Borth, Jennie Forsberg, Grace Hansen

Design Contributors: Christina Doffing, Candice Keimig, Dorothy Toth

Publisher's Cataloging-in-Publication Data

Names: Murray, Julie, author.

Title: Badgers / by Julie Murray.

Description: Minneapolis, Minnesota : Abdo Kids, 2018. | Series: Nocturnal animals |
        Includes glossary, index and online resource (page 24).

Identifiers: LCCN 2017908178 | ISBN 9781532104053 (lib.bdg.) | ISBN 9781532105173 (ebook) |
        ISBN 9781532105739 (Read-to-me ebook)

Subjects: LCSH: Badgers--North America--Juvenile literature. | Nocturnal animals--Juvenile literature.

Classification: DDC 599.767--dc23

LC record available at https://lccn.loc.gov/2017908178

Table of Contents

Badgers

The sun goes down. Badgers wake up. They are ready to hunt!

Badgers live around the world.

Many are found in **grasslands**.

Their homes are underground.

They are called **setts**.

They have long noses.

They have short legs.

12

Their faces are black and white. There are stripes on their heads.

They have sharp claws.

These help dig for food.

They like to eat worms. They also eat small animals.

They can live for 10 years.

Features of Badgers

black and white face

long nose

sharp claws

short legs

Glossary

grassland
a large open area covered in grass with very few trees.

setts
the lair or burrow of a badger.

Index

Abdo Kids
ONLINE
FREE! ONLINE MULTIMEDIA RESOURCES

Visit **abdokids.com** and use this code to access crafts, games, videos, and more!

Abdo Kids Code:
NBK4053